YOU'RE
TO LOV

GOING
E THIS!

OXFORD

UNIVERSITY PRESS

Great Clarendon Street, Oxford OX2 6DP

Oxford University Press is a department of the University of Oxford.
It furthers the University's objective of excellence in research, scholarship,
and education by publishing worldwide in

Oxford New York

Auckland Cape Town Dar es Salaam Hong Kong Karachi
Kuala Lumpur Madrid Melbourne Mexico City Nairobi
New Delhi Shanghai Taipei Toronto

Oxford is a registered trade mark of Oxford University Press
in the UK and in certain other countries

British Library Cataloguing in Publication Data available

ISBN-13: 978-0-19-276275-7
ISBN-10: 0-19-276275-3

5 7 9 10 8 6 4

Typeset by Mary Tudge (Typesetting Services)
in Twinkle, Joanna, and Stone Sans

Printed in Singapore

My First Oxford Book of NONSENSE POEMS

CLANG

Compiled by
John Foster

OXFORD
UNIVERSITY PRESS

Contents

The Spangled Pandemonium

In the Land of Rumplydoodle

The Man From the Land of Fandango

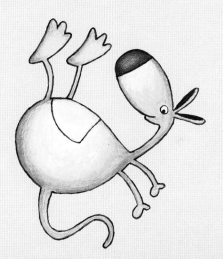

The Owl and the Pussy-Cat

The Dancing Carrot

When Fishes Set Umbrellas Up

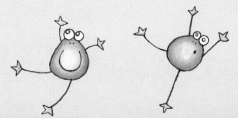

The Spangled Pandemonium

The spangled pandemonium
Is missing from the zoo.
He bent the bars the barest bit,
And slithered glibly through.

He crawled across the moated wall,
He climbed the mango tree,
And when the keeper scrambled up,
He nipped him in the knee.

To all of you, a warning
Not to wander after dark,
Or if you must, make very sure
You stay out of the park.

For the spangled pandemonium
Is missing from the zoo,
And since he nipped his keeper,
He would just as soon nip you.

Palmer Brown

The Spangled Pandemonium

I wish I was a little grub

I wish I was a little grub
With whiskers round my tummy.
I'd climb into a honey-pot
And make my tummy gummy.
And then I'd crawl all over you
And make your tummy gummy, too.

Anon.

My TV came down with a chill

My TV came down with a chill.
As soon as I saw it was ill
   I wrapped up its channels
   In warm winter flannels
And gave its antenna a pill.

Willard R. Espy

A Wasp on a Nettle Said: 'Coo!'

A wasp on a nettle said: 'Coo!
We're in a right mess, me and you.
    We have got to sort out
    What this is about.
Please tell me—who's got to sting who?'

Frank Richards

A Wisp of a Wasp

I'm a wisp of a wasp with a worry,
I'm hiding somewhere in Surrey
I've just bit upon
The fat sit upon
    of the King—so I left in a hurry.

Colin West

The Jumblies

They went to sea in a Sieve, they did,
 In a Sieve they went to sea;
In spite of all their friends could say,
On a winter's morn, on a stormy day,
 In a Sieve they went to sea!
And when the Sieve turned round and round,
And everyone cried, 'You'll all be drowned!'
They called aloud, 'Our Sieve ain't big,
But we don't care a button, we don't care a fig!
 In a Sieve we'll go to sea.'
  Far and few, far and few,
   Are the lands where the Jumblies live;
   Their heads are green, and their hands are blue,
    And they went to sea in a Sieve.

They sailed away in a Sieve, they did,
 In a Sieve they sailed so fast;
With only a beautiful pea-green veil
Tied with a riband by way of a sail
 To a small tobacco-pipe mast;
And everyone said, who saw them go,
'O won't they be soon upset, you know,
For the sky is dark, and the voyage is long,
And happen what may, it's extremely wrong,
 In a Sieve to sail so fast.'
  Far and few, far and few,
   Are the lands where the Jumblies live;
   Their heads are green, and their hands are blue,
    And they went to sea in a Sieve.

The water it soon came in, it did,
  The water it soon came in;
So to keep them dry, they wrapped their feet
In a pinky paper, all folded neat,
  And they fastened it down with a pin.
And they passed the night in a crockery jar,
And each of them said, 'How wise we are!
Though the sky be dark and the voyage be long
Yet we never can think we were rash or wrong,
  While round in our Sieve we spin!'
    Far and few, far and few,
      Are the lands where the Jumblies live;
    Their heads are green, and their hands are blue,
      And they went to sea in a Sieve.

And all night long they sailed away;
   And when the sun went down,
They whistled and warbled a moony song,
To the echoing sound of a coppery gong,
   In the shade of the mountains brown.
'O Timballo! How happy we are,
When we live in a Sieve and a crockery jar,
And all night long in the moonlight pale,
We sail away with a pea-green sail
   In the shade of the mountains brown!'
     Far and few, far and few,
       Are the lands where the Jumblies live;
      Their heads are green, and their hands are blue,
       And they went to sea in a Sieve.

They sailed to the Western Sea, they did,
    To a land all covered with trees,
And they bought an Owl and a useful Cart,
And a pound of Rice and a Cranberry Tart,
    And a hive of silvery Bees.
And they bought a Pig, and some green Jack-daws,
And a lovely Monkey with lollipop paws,
And forty bottles of Ring-Bo-Ree,
    And no end of Stilton Cheese.
        Far and few, far and few,
            Are the lands where the Jumblies live;
        Their heads are green, and their hands are blue,
            And they went to sea in a Sieve.

And in twenty years they all came back,
    In twenty years or more.
And everyone said, 'How tall they've grown!
For they've been to the Lakes, and the Torrible Zone,
    And the hills of the Chankly Bore;'
And they drank their health and gave them a feast
Of dumplings made of beautiful yeast;
And everyone said, 'If we only live,
We, too, will go to sea in a Sieve—
    To the hills of the Chankly Bore!'
        Far and few, far and few,
            Are the lands where the Jumblies live;
        Their heads are green, and their hands are blue,
            And they went to sea in a Sieve.

Edward Lear

A Woobit Song

A Woobit went walking through Carraway Town
In his ragged new sweater and his tin golden crown.
He whiffled and wurbled and sang 'worrajee',
Because he was coming to eat me for tea.

He woffed on the doorstep and wonged on the bell,
He sniggled and snorfed at the thought of the smell
Of little girl chops and little girl pies,
(He wanted to crunch me with vinegary fries).

But I didn't care for his scrobbles and squeals,
(Because *nobody* likes to be Woobitses' meals).
So I tromped on his crown, and wurfulled his sweater,
And now (for a Woobit) he couldn't be better.

Lucy Coats

The elephant knocked the ground

The elephant knocked the ground with a stick,
He knocked it slow, he knocked it quick.
He knocked it till his trunk turned black—
Then the ground turned round and knocked him back.

Adrian Mitchell

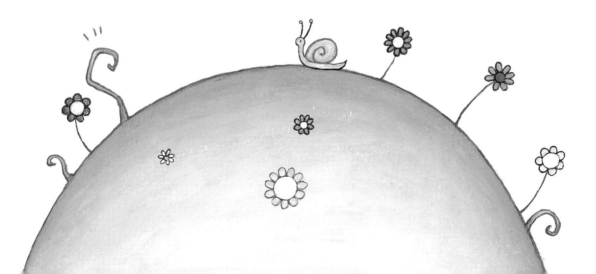

Jabberwocky

'Twas brillig, and the slithy toves
    Did gyre and gimble in the wabe:
All mimsy were the borogoves,
    And the mome raths outgrabe.

'Beware the Jabberwock, my son!
    The jaws that bite, the claws that catch!
Beware the Jubjub bird, and shun
    The frumious Bandersnatch!'

He took his vorpal sword in hand:
    Long time the manxome foe he sought—
So rested he by the Tumtum tree,
    And stood awhile in thought.

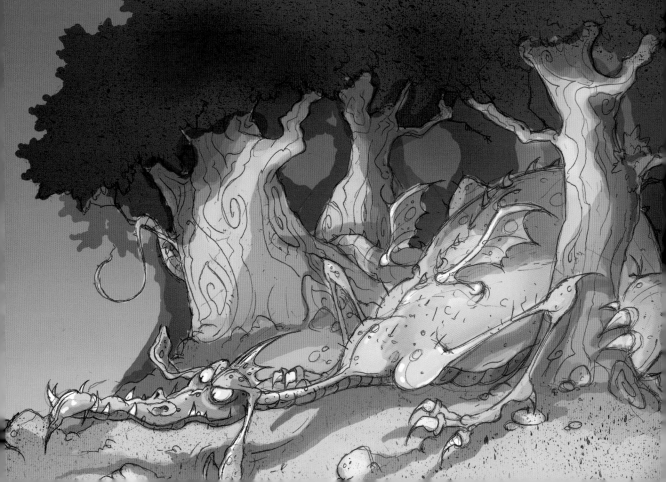

And, as in uffish thought he stood,
    The Jabberwock, with eyes of flame,
Came whiffling through the tulgey wood,
    And burbled as it came!

One, two! One, two! And through and through
    The vorpal blade went snicker-snack!
He left it dead, and with its head
    He went galumphing back.

'And hast thou slain the Jabberwock?
    Come to my arms, my beamish boy!
O frabjous day! Callooh! Callay!'
    He chortled in his joy.

'Twas brillig, and the slithy toves
    Did gyre and gimble in the wabe:
All mimsy were the borogoves,
    And the mome raths outgrabe.

Lewis Carroll

Bigtrousers Dan

In the land of Rumplydoodle
where men eat jollips for tea,
and the cows in the hay
feel sleepy all day,
there's a wonderful sight to see.
On the banks of the River Bongbong,
in a hut made of turnips and cream,
sits a whiskery man,
name of Bigtrousers Dan,
and he plays with his brand new machine.
There are gronfles
and nogglets
and pluffles
and valves that go
ker-pling and ker-plang,
and a big sugar wheel
that revolves with a squeal
till it's oiled with a chocolate meringue.
There are wurdlies
and flumdings
and crumchies
that go round just as fast as they can,
and a big chocolate ball
that makes no sound at all,
thanks to clever old
Bigtrousers Dan.

Peter Mortimer

22

In the Land of Rumplydoodle

If Pigs Could Fly

If Pigs could fly, I'd fly a pig
To foreign countries small and big—
   To Italy and Spain,
To Austria, where cowbells ring,
To Germany, where people sing—
   And then come home again.

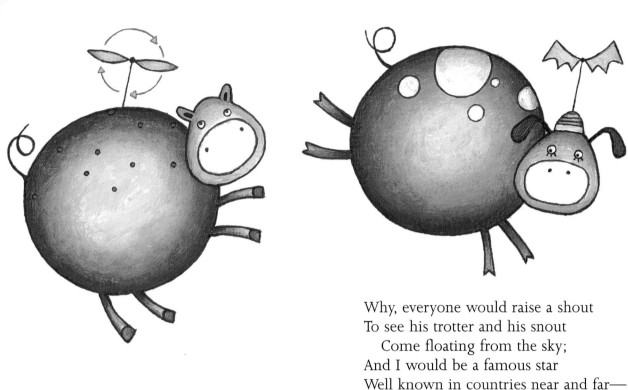

Why, everyone would raise a shout
To see his trotter and his snout
    Come floating from the sky;
And I would be a famous star
Well known in countries near and far—
    If only pigs could fly!

James Reeves

I'd see the Ganges and the Nile:
I'd visit Madagascar's isle,
    And Persia and Peru.
People would say they'd never seen
So odd, so strange an air-machine
    As that on which I flew.

25

Humpty Dumpty Went to the Moon

Humpty Dumpty went to the moon
on a supersonic spoon.
He took some porridge and a tent
but when he landed
the spoon got bent.
Humpty said he didn't care
and for all I know
he's still up there.

Michael Rosen

If I Were An Explorer

If I were an explorer
I'd reach that far-off land
Called Jumbledup, where sand was sea
And sea was made of sand,
Where snow fell every summer
On herds of grazing bees,
And cows flew round the blossom
Of the orange apple trees.

Richard Edwards

The Sugar-Plum Tree

Have you ever heard of the Sugar-Plum Tree?
'Tis a marvel of great renown!
It blooms on the shore of the Lollipop sea
In the garden of Shut-Eye Town;
The fruit that it bears is so wondrously sweet
(As those who have tasted it say)
That good little children have only to eat
Of that fruit to be happy next day.

When you've got to the tree, you would have a hard time
To capture the fruit which I sing;
The tree is so tall that no person could climb
To the boughs where the sugar-plums swing!
But up in that tree sits a chocolate cat,
And a gingerbread dog prowls below—
And this is the way you contrive to get at
Those sugar-plums tempting you so:

You say but the word to that gingerbread dog
And he barks with such terrible zest
That the chocolate cat is at once all agog,
As her swelling proportions attest.

And the chocolate cat goes cavorting around
From this leafy limb unto that,
And the sugar-plums, tumble, of course, to the ground—
Hurrah for that chocolate cat!

There are marshmallows, gumdrops, and peppermint canes,
With stripings of scarlet or gold,
And you carry away of the treasure that rains
As much as your apron can hold!
So come, little child, cuddle closer to me
In your dainty white nightcap and gown,
And I'll rock you away to that Sugar-Plum Tree
In the garden of Shut-Eye Town.

Eugene Field

The Quangle Wangle's Hat

On top of the Crumpetty Tree
   The Quangle Wangle sat,
But his face you could not see,
   On account of his Beaver Hat.
For his Hat was a hundred and two feet wide,
With ribbons and bibbons on every side,
And bells, and buttons, and loops, and lace,
So that nobody ever could see the face
     Of the Quangle Wangle Quee.

The Quangle Wangle said
   To himself on the Crumpetty Tree,
'Jam; and jelly; and bread;
   Are the best of food for me!
But the longer I live on this Crumpetty Tree,
The plainer than ever it seems to me
That very few people come this way,
And that life on the whole is far from gay!
     Said the Quangle Wangle Quee.

But there came to the Crumpetty Tree
   Mr and Mrs Canary;
And they said, 'Did ever you see
   Any spot so charmingly airy?
May we build a nest on your lovely Hat?
Mr Quangle Wangle, grant us that!
O please let us come and build a nest
Of whatever material suits you best,
     Mr Quangle Wangle Quee!'

And besides, to the Crumpetty Tree
   Came the Stork, the Duck, and the Owl;
The Snail and the Bumble-Bee,
   The Frog, and the Fimble Fowl
(The Fimble Fowl with a corkscrew leg);
And all of them said, 'We humbly beg,
We may build our homes on your lovely Hat,
Mr Quangle Wangle, grant us that!
    Mr Quangle Wangle Quee!'

And the Golden Grouse came there,
   And the Pobble who hast no toes,
And the small Olympian Bear
   And the Dong with a luminous nose.
And the Blue Baboon, who played the flute,
And the Orient Calf from the Land of Tute,
And the Attery Squash and the Bisky Bat,
All came and built on the lovely Hat
    Of the Quangle Wangle Quee.

And the Quangle Wangle said
   To himself on the Crumpetty Tree,
'When all these creatures move
   What a wonderful noise there'll be!'
And at night by the light of the Mulberry Moon
They danced to the Flute of the Blue Baboon
On the broad green leaves of the Crumpetty Tree,
And all were as happy as happy could be,
    With the Quangle Wangle Quee.

Edward Lear

31

BONG

BONG

32

On the Ning Nang Nong

On the Ning Nang Nong
Where the cows go Bong!
And the monkeys all say Boo!
There's a Nong Nang Ning
Where the trees go Ping!
And the tea-pots Jibber Jabber Joo!
On the Nong Ning Nang
All the mice go Clang!
And you just can't catch 'em when they do!
So it's Ning Nang Nong!
Cows go Bong!
Nong Nang Ning!
Trees go Ping!
Nong Ning Nang!
The mice go Clang!
What a noisy place to belong
Is the Ning Nang Ning Nang Nong!

Spike Milligan

33

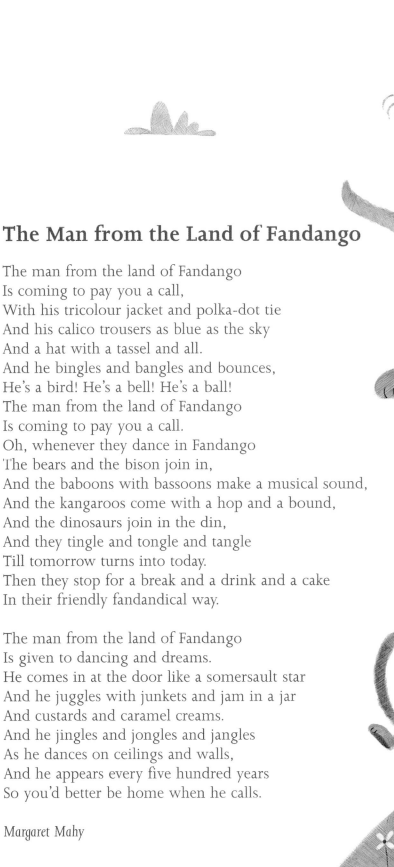

The Man from the Land of Fandango

The man from the land of Fandango
Is coming to pay you a call,
With his tricolour jacket and polka-dot tie
And his calico trousers as blue as the sky
And a hat with a tassel and all.
And he bingles and bangles and bounces,
He's a bird! He's a bell! He's a ball!
The man from the land of Fandango
Is coming to pay you a call.
Oh, whenever they dance in Fandango
The bears and the bison join in,
And the baboons with bassoons make a musical sound,
And the kangaroos come with a hop and a bound,
And the dinosaurs join in the din,
And they tingle and tongle and tangle
Till tomorrow turns into today.
Then they stop for a break and a drink and a cake
In their friendly fandandical way.

The man from the land of Fandango
Is given to dancing and dreams.
He comes in at the door like a somersault star
And he juggles with junkets and jam in a jar
And custards and caramel creams.
And he jingles and jongles and jangles
As he dances on ceilings and walls,
And he appears every five hundred years
So you'd better be home when he calls.

Margaret Mahy

34

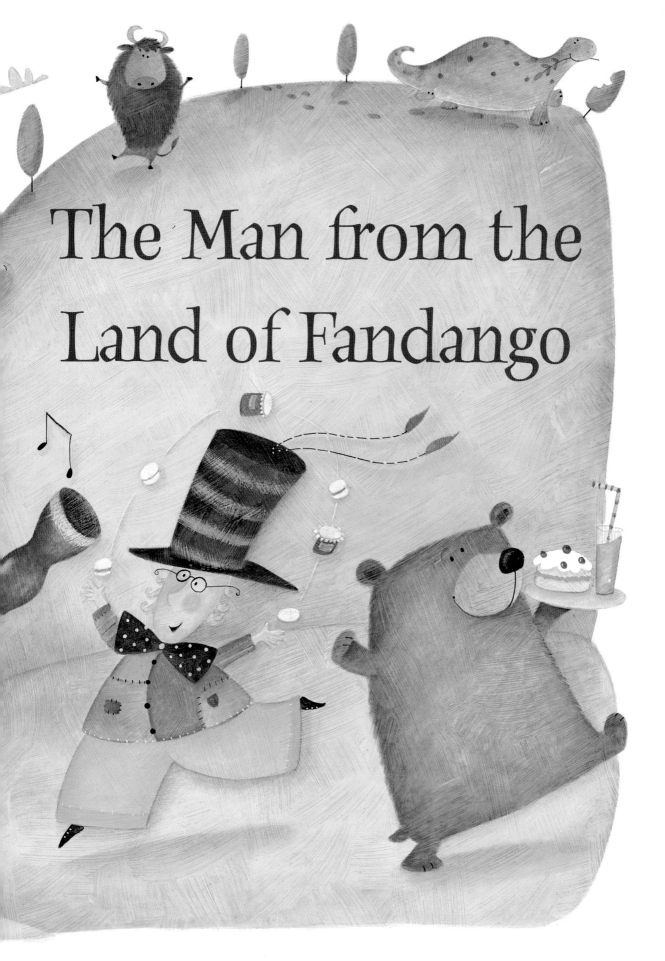

The Man from the Land of Fandango

Cincinnati Patty

Cincinnati Patty,
smaller than a thumb,
rode a mouse to Cleveland
to feast upon a plum,
she feasted for a minute,
and that was her mistake,
for Cincinnati Patty
got a giant belly ache.

Jack Prelutsky

My Cousin, an Explorer Called Betty

My cousin, an explorer called Betty
Grew fat eating plates of spaghetti.
On a trek in Tibet,
She was caught in a net
And displayed in the zoo as a Yeti.

Gervase Phinn

The Gondoliers of Greenland

The Gondoliers of Greenland
Are the Grumpiest folk in the North
Their canals melt on August the Second
And freeze up on August the Fourth.
In those two laborious glorious days
All their incomes must be made
And the rest of the year they wait listlessly
To ply their ridiculous trade.

Adrian Mitchell

Mabel Murple

Mabel Murple's house was purple
So was Mabel's hair
Mabel Murple's cat was purple
Purple everywhere.

Mabel Murple's bike was purple
So were Mabel's ears
And when Mabel Murple cried
She cried terrible purple tears.

Sheree Fitch

Chester's Undoing

Chester Lester Kirkenby Dale
Caught his sweater on a nail.
As Chester Lester started to travel
So his sweater began to unravel.
A great long trail of crinkly wool
Followed Chester down to school.
Then his ears unravelled!
His neck and his nose!
Chester undid from his head
To his toes.
Chester's undone, one un-purl, two un-plain,
Who's got the pattern to knit him again?

Julie Holder

Sir Smasham Uppe

Good afternoon, Sir Smasham Uppe!
We're having tea: do take a cup.
Sugar and milk? Now let me see—
Two lumps, I think? . . . Good gracious me!
The silly thing slipped off your knee!
Pray don't apologize, old chap:
A very trivial mishap!
So clumsy of you? How absurd!
My dear Sir Smasham, not a word!
Now do sit down and have another,
And tell us all about your brother—
You know, the one who broke his head.
Is the poor fellow still in bed?—
A chair—allow me, sir! . . . Great Scott!
That *was* a nasty smash! Eh, what?
Oh, not at all: the chair was old—
Queen Anne, or so we have been told.

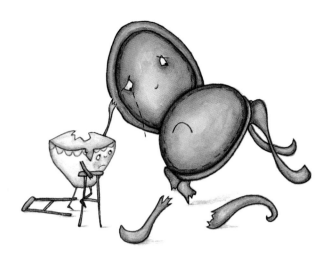

We've got at least a dozen more:
Just leave the pieces on the floor.
I want you to admire our view:
Come nearer to the window, do;
And look how beautiful . . . Tut, tut!
You didn't see that it was shut?
I hope you are not badly cut!
Not hurt? A fortunate escape!
Amazing! Not a single scrape!
And now, if you have finished tea,
I fancy you might like to see
A little thing or two I've got.
That china plate? Yes, worth a lot:
A beauty too . . . Ah, there it goes!
I trust it didn't hurt your toes?
Your elbow brushed it off the shelf?
Of course: I've done the same myself.
And now, my dear Sir Smasham—Oh,
You surely don't intend to go?
You must be off? Well, come again.
So glad you're fond of porcelain!

E.V. Rieu

Little John was not content

Little John was not content
Unless he played with wet cement.
    One day alas in someone's yard,
    He stayed too long and set quite hard.
His mother didn't want him home
So now he's just a garden gnome.

Max Fatchen

As I Was Going Out One Day

As I was going out one day
My head fell off and rolled away.
But when I saw that it was gone,
I picked it up and put it on.

And when I got into the street
A fellow cried: 'Look at your feet!'
I looked at them and sadly said:
'I've left them both asleep in bed!'

Anon.

Uncle Ed's Heads

Fame was a claim of Uncle Ed's,
Simply because he had three heads,
Which, if he'd only had a third of,
I think he would never have been heard of.

Ogden Nash

There Was an Old Man With a Beard

There was an old Man with a beard,
Who said, 'It is just as I feared!—
Two Owls and a Hen,
Four Larks and a Wren
Have all built their nests in my beard!'

Edward Lear

43

Mr Pennycomequick

Mr Hector Pennycomequick
   Stood on the castle keep,
Opened up a carriage-umbrella
   And took a mighty leap.

'Hooray!' cried Mr Pennycomequick
   As he went through the air.
'I've always wanted to go like this
   From here to Newport Square.'

But Mr Hector Pennycomequick
   He never did float nor fly.
He landed in an ivy-bush
   His legs up in the sky.

Mr Hector Pennycomequick
   They hurried home to bed
With a bump the size of a seagull's egg
   On the top of his head.

'So sorry,' said Mr Pennycomequick,
   'For causing all this fuss.
When next I go to Newport Square
   I think I'll take the bus.'

The moral of this little tale
   Is difficult to refute:
A carriage-umbrella's a carriage-umbrella
   And not a parachute.

Charles Causley

Valerie Malory and Sue Hu Nu

Valerie Malory and Sue Hu Nu
Went to school on a kangaroo
Halfway there and halfway back
They met a duck with half a quack.

Valerie Malory and Sue Hu Nu
Arrived at school with a kangaroo
Halfway there and halfway in
They met a cat with half a grin.

Valerie Malory and Sue Hu Nu
Came home from school on a kangaroo
Halfway here and halfway there
They met a clown with half a chair.

Valerie Malory and Sue Hu Nu
Went upstairs on a kangaroo
Halfway up and halfway down
They met a king with half a crown.

Valerie Malory and Sue Hu Nu
Went to bed with a kangaroo
Half asleep and half awake
They dreamt of a . . . duck and a quack
    and a grin and a cat
        and a king and a clown
            and a chair and a crown
                and a kangaroo
                    with half a shoe.

Trevor Millum

My Uncle Paul of Pimlico

My Uncle Paul of Pimlico
Has seven cats as white as snow,
Who sit at his enormous feet
And watch him, as a special treat,
Play the piano upside-down,
In his delightful dressing gown;
The firelight leaps, the parlour glows,
And, while the music ebbs and flows,
They smile (while purring the refrains),
At little thoughts that cross their brains.

Mervyn Peake

Uncle Ben from Number One

Uncle Ben was not a hen
But when he laid an egg
He did it quite professionally
By lifting up a leg.

He studied it and prodded it
And said, 'I'm mystified.'
And then he took it to the kitchen
Where he had it, fried.

Brian Patten

The Owl and the Pussy-Cat

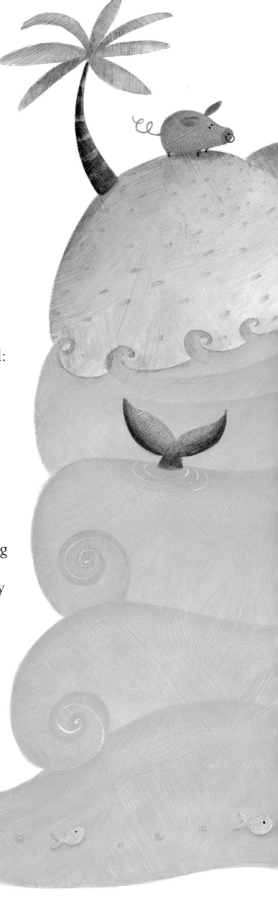

The Owl and the Pussy-cat went to sea
   In a beautiful pea-green boat:
They took some honey and plenty of money
   Wrapped up in a five-pound note.
The Owl looked up to the stars above,
   And sang to a small guitar,
'O lovely Pussy, O Pussy, my love,
   What a beautiful Pussy you are,
     You are,
     You are!
   What a beautiful Pussy you are!'

Pussy said to the Owl, 'You elegant fowl,
   How charmingly sweet you sing!
Oh! let us be married; too long we have tarried:
   But what shall we do for a ring?'
They sailed away for a year and a day,
   To the land where the bong-tree grows;
And there in a wood a Piggy-wig stood,
   With a ring at the end of his nose,
     His nose,
     His nose,
   With a ring at the end of his nose.

'Dear Pig, are you willing to sell for one shilling
   Your ring?' Said the Piggy, 'I will.'
So they took it away, and were married next day
   By the Turkey who lives on the hill.
They dined on mince and slices of quince,
   Which they ate with a runcible spoon;
And hand in hand, on the edge of the sand,
   They danced by the light of the moon,
     The moon,
     The moon,
   They danced by the light of the moon.

Edward Lear

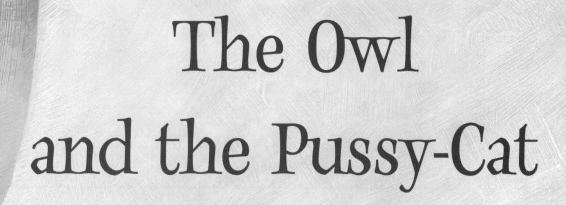

The Owl
and the Pussy-Cat

A Frog and a Flea

A frog and a flea
And a kangaroo
Once jumped for a prize
In a pot of glue;
The kangaroo stuck
And so did the flea,
And the frog limped home
With a fractured knee.

Cynthia Mitchell

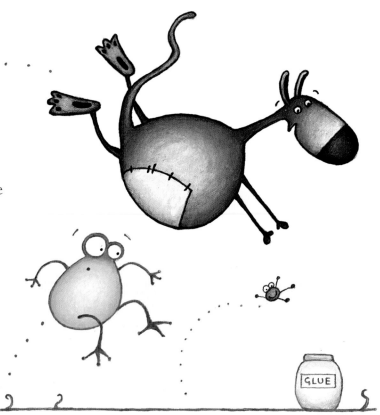

The Donkey

I had a Donkey, that was all right,
But he always wanted to fly my Kite;
Every time I let him, the String would bust.
Your Donkey is better behaved I trust.

Theodore Roethke

The Llamas' Holiday

A bunch of adventurous llamas
Dressed up in bright coloured pyjamas
　　And set off one night
　　On a holiday flight
To a beach in the balmy Bahamas.

They didn't enjoy themselves fully:
When they swam they were heavy and woolly—
　　And they might have all drowned,
　　But the lifeguard came round
And hoisted them out with a pulley!

Gordon Snell

The Ants at the Olympics

At last year's Jungle Olympics,
the Ants were completely outclassed.
In fact, from an entry of sixty-two teams,
the Ants came their usual last.

They didn't win one single medal.
Not that that's a surprise.
The reason was not lack of trying,
but more their unfortunate size.

While the cheetahs won most of the sprinting
and the hippos won putting the shot,
the Ants tried sprinting but couldn't,
and tried to put but could not.

It was sad for the Ants 'cause they're sloggers.
They turn out for every event.
With their shorts and their bright orange T-shirts,
their athletes are proud they are sent.

They came last at the high jump and hurdles,
which they say they'd have won, but they fell.
They came last in the four hundred metres
and last in the swimming as well.

They came last in long distance running,
though they say they might have come first.
And they might if the other sixty-one teams
hadn't put in a finishing burst.

But each year they turn up regardless.
They're popular in the parade.
The other teams whistle and cheer them,
aware of the journey they've made.

For the Jungle Olympics in August,
they have to set off New Year's Day.
They didn't arrive the year before last.
They set off but went the wrong way.

So long as they try there's a reason.
After all, it's only a sport.
They'll be back next year to bring up the rear,
and that's an encouraging thought.

Richard Digance

53

Hippopotabus

The harmless hippopotabus,
　　Is lots of fun for all of us;
He lets the children hop inside
　　And charges nothing for a ride.

Doug McLeod

The Bison

The Bison is vain and (I write it with pain)
The Door-Mat you see on his head
Is not, as some learned professors maintain,
The opulent growth of a genius' brain;
But is sewn on with needle and thread.

Hilaire Belloc

A Sea-Serpent Saw a Big Tanker

A sea-serpent saw a big tanker,
Bit a hole in her side and then sank her.
  It swallowed the crew
  In a minute or two,
And then picked its teeth with the anchor.

Anon.

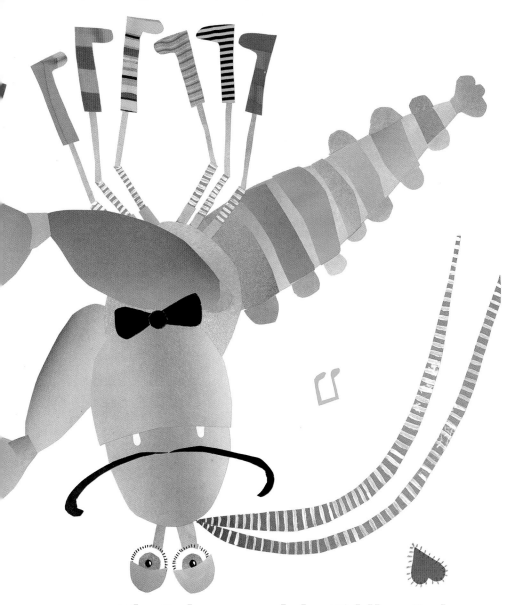

The Lobsters and the Fiddler Crab

The lobsters came ashore one night
    In the merry month of June,
And coaxed the fiddler crab to play
    A rollicking tango tune.

The lobsters danced, the fiddler played
    Till morning, rosy red,
Chased the dancers into the sea
    And the fiddler home to bed!

Frederick J. Forster

The Waltzing Polar Bears

While the snowy owl hoots and the Arctic fox wails,
The polar bear waltzes
In white tie and tails.

His top hat gets tilted as he spins around twice,
His long claws go rattling
Over the ice.

The Northern Lights up in the heavens glow down
As his partner appears
In a shimmering gown.

Reflected in glaciers, they dance jaw-to-jaw
Through the hail and the blizzard
And the hurricane's roar.

He wheels her around on her sparkling slippers
While the seals and penguins
Applaud with their flippers.

And squawk in amazement and bark with delight
At the polar bears waltzing
Through the long Arctic night.

Andrew Matthews

Octopus

It's quite a lengthy business
When an octopus gets dressed.
He likes his trousers ironed,
He likes them creased and pressed.
And dressing for an octopus
Is not a lot of fun,
There's eight black socks and eight black shoes,
And laces to be done.

Oh, it's quite a lengthy business
When an octopus eats food.
With eight elbows on the table
He's eight times very rude
He grabs eight cream buns, and eight mince tarts,
And seaweed minced and stewed,
And he always eats at eight o'clock,
When he's eight times in the mood . . .

Clive Riche

A Fishy Tale

A haddock sat in a shoe shop
Surrounded by dozens of shoes.
'Oh dear,' he sighed,
'What a fix I am in.
I just don't know
Which pair I should choose.'

'Don't worry, dear sir,'
The assistant replied,
'For as you've no feet it is plain,
That a pair of shoes
Will be no use at all
When you're back in the ocean again.

'But a folding umbrella
That's sturdy and light,
I strongly advise you to buy.
For then when it rains
You can swim all day long
And keep your hair perfectly dry.'

Cynthia Rider

The Shark

Oh, blithe and merrily sang the shark
As he sat on the house top high,
A-cleaning his boots and smoking cheroots,
With a single glass in his eye.

He sang so loud he astonished the crowd,
Which gathered from far and near;
For they said, 'Such a sound in the country 'round
We never—no never did hear.'

He sang of ships he'd eaten like chips,
In the palmy days of his youth;
And he added, 'If you don't believe that it's true,
Pray examine my wisdom tooth!'

He sang of whales who'd given their tails
For a glance of his raven eye;
And the swordfish, too, who their weapons drew,
And vowed for his sake they'd die.

He sang about wrecks and hurricane decks,
And the mariner's perils and pains;
Till every man's blood up on end it stood,
And their hair ran cold in their veins.

But blithe as a lark the merry old shark
Sat on the sloping roof;
Though he said, 'It's queer that no one draws near
To examine my wisdom tooth!'

He carolled by night and by day,
Until he made everyone ill;
And I'll wager a crown that unless he's come down
He is probably carolling still.

Laura E. Richards

The Dancing Carrot

The beetroot was getting married,
The celery squealed with delight
The carrot stood up to dance a jig,
And the horseradish whistled all night.

Traditional Czech, translated by Andrew Fusek Peters

The Dancing Carrot

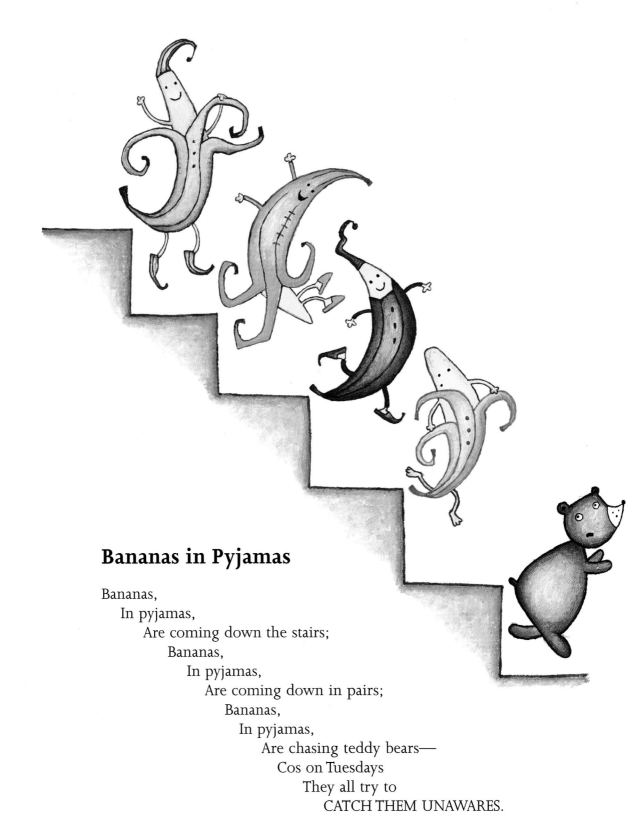

Bananas in Pyjamas

Bananas,
   In pyjamas,
      Are coming down the stairs;
     Bananas,
       In pyjamas,
        Are coming down in pairs;
      Bananas,
       In pyjamas,
        Are chasing teddy bears—
       Cos on Tuesdays
       They all try to
        CATCH THEM UNAWARES.

Carey Blyton

One day a boy went walking

One day a boy went walking
And walked into a store;
He bought a pound of sausages
And laid them on the floor.

The boy began to whistle
A merry little tune—
And all the little sausages
Danced around the room!

Anon.

Beans

It's bad out there
it's scary, it's weird
you thought it was hard
but it's worse than you feared.

Next time they say it'll be 'cloudy'
do you know what that really means?
Yes, of course it's going to rain
but it's going to rain baked beans.

Millions and millions of beans
are going to fall out of the sky
all over me and you
I promise you this is no lie.

The streets will be covered with beans;
over houses and cars and vans.
Your hair will be sticky with beans
there'll be beans all over your hands.

Towers will drip with the juice.
Houses will all disappear.
It's going to be something that lasts
for anything up to a year.

Bulldozers will be called into action;
they'll try to move the muck,
but after just a few minutes
most of them will be stuck.

People will go out with hoses;
buckets, jugs, and cups
and hundreds of hungry people
will try to gobble it up.

It'll take ten years in all
to clean up every little bean.
So remember—next time you hear the
          word 'cloudy'
you know what it will mean.

Michael Rosen

The Midnight Skaters

It is midnight in the ice-rink
   And all is cool and still.
Darkness seems to hold its breath
   Nothing moves, until

Out of the kitchen, one by one,
   The cutlery comes creeping,
Quiet as mice to the brink of the ice
   While all the world is sleeping.

Then suddenly, a serving-spoon
   Switches on the light,
And the silver swoops upon the ice
   Screaming with delight.

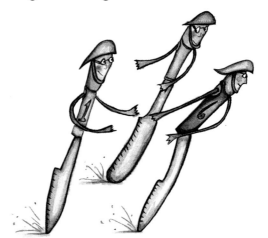

The knives are high-speed skaters
   Round and round they race,
Blades hissing, sissing,
   Whizzing at a dizzy pace.

Forks twirl like dancers
Pirouetting on the spot.
Teaspoons (who take no chances)
Hold hands and giggle a lot.

All night long the fun goes on
Until the sun, their friend,
Gives the warning signal
That all good things must end.

So they slink back to the darkness
Of the kitchen cutlery-drawer
And steel themselves to wait
Until it's time to skate once more.

At eight the canteen ladies
Breeze in as good as gold
To lay the tables and wonder
Why the cutlery is so cold.

Roger McGough

71

I eat my peas with honey

I eat my peas with honey,
I've done it all my life.
It makes the peas taste funny,
But it keeps them on the knife.

Anon.

Simple Simon Bought a Pie

Simple Simon bought a pie,
But when he took a bite
A caterpillar wriggled out
To spoil his appetite.

Richard Edwards

Snowflake Soufflé

Snowflake soufflé,
Snowflake soufflé
Makes a lip-smacking lunch
On an ice-cold day.

You take seven snowflakes,
You break seven eggs,
And you stir it seven times
With your two hind legs.

Bake it in an igloo,
Throw it on a plate,
And slice off a slice
With a rusty ice-skate.

X. J. Kennedy

Uncle Ted's Tea

The table was laid and ready
For the visit of Uncle Ted,
When a horse looked in at the window
And whinnied a bit and said:

'I've come to make his excuses,
Your Uncle Ted can't come.
He fell off a chair last Thursday
And his ears have gone all numb.

But if those are crumpets I see
Behind that yellow cup,
I'll step inside and assist you
To eat the whole lot up.'

Before we could speak or stop him
He was seated and tucking in,
He finished not only the crumpets
But the plates and the biscuit tin.

Then he smacked his lips and snickered
And went galloping out of the door,
Leaving us only some horse hairs
And his hoof prints on the floor.

A few minutes later the bell rang
And outside stood Uncle Ted
Smiling and stout on the doorstep,
'I hope I'm not late,' he said.

We explained that the cupboard was empty,
That there wasn't a bite in the place.
'That horse has been here. I knew it!'
He cried going red in the face.

'Was he piebald and thin?' We nodded.
'That's Humphrey,' he groaned in disgust.
'He promised to be my best friend,
A creature I could trust.'

Then he turned away and left us,
Tut-tutting and shaking his head,
And he never comes round to tea now,
He comes to lunch instead.

So remember this little story,
There's a moral here, of course:
If you're asked out to tea and there's crumpets—
Don't ever tell a horse.

Richard Edwards

When Fishes Set Umbrellas Up

When fishes set umbrellas up
   If the rain-drops run,
Lizards will want their parasols
   To shade them from the sun.

The peacock has a score of eyes,
   With which he cannot see;
The cod-fish has a silent sound,
   However that may be.

No dandelions tell the time
   Although they turn to clocks;
Cat's cradle does not hold the cat,
   Nor foxglove fit the fox.

Christina Rossetti

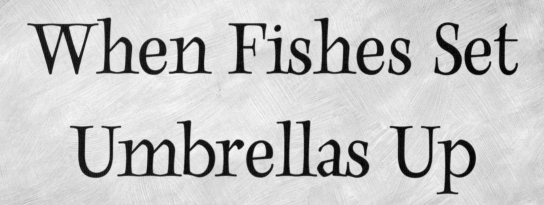

When Fishes Set Umbrellas Up

Mad Weather We're Having

It's raining cats and dogs again,
It said so on the news.
Last Sunday it rained penguins.
On Monday, kangaroos.

On Tuesday, it was froggy,
On Wednesday, cold as mice,
On Thursday, it snowed polar bears
(Which wasn't very nice).

Friday was a fowl day,
Saturday was bats,
And now we're back to Sunday
With a load more dogs and cats.

I'd like to stay here talking
But I'm soaked right to the skin.
Now it's blowing up a buffalo!
I think I'm going in.

Kaye Umansky

'Twas in the Month of Liverpool

'Twas in the month of Liverpool
In the city of July,
The snow was raining heavily,
The streets were very dry.
The flowers were sweetly singing,
The birds were in full bloom,
As I went down to the cellar
To sweep an upstairs room.

Anon.

A Dream

I dreamed a dream next Tuesday week,
Beneath the apple-trees;
I thought my eyes were big pork-pies,
And my nose was Stilton cheese.

The clock struck twenty minutes to six,
When a frog sat on my knee;
I asked him to lend me eighteen pence
But he borrowed a shilling of me.

Anon.

The Girl with the Marmalade Hair

Whoosh went the wind
and up in the air
went a very small girl
with marmalade hair.

Boom went the wind
and a pig passing by
joined the small marmalade
girl in the sky.

They tumbled like leaves,
a peculiar pair.
'Hello,' said the girl
with the marmalade hair.

'Hello,' said the pig.
'Strange to travel like this,
but delightful to know
such a marmalade miss.'

'If we fly off to China
and back; we don't care,'
cried the pig and the girl
with the marmalade hair.

Marian Swinger

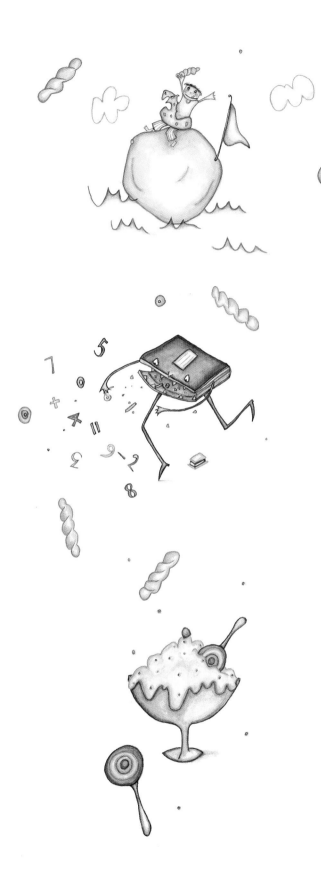

Dog's Dinner

On Thursday night
my mother said
that I could sleep
in the barley-sugar bed.

I dreamed of sailing
a bubble-gum boat
blown big as a dinosaur
to keep me afloat.

On Friday night
my mother said
my sister could sleep
in the barley-sugar bed.

She dreamed of
a liquorice homework book
that ate the sums
when she was stuck.

On Saturday
my mother said
she would like to sleep
in the barley-sugar bed.

She dreamed of
a trifle covered in cream
with lollipop spoons
to lick it clean.

When Sunday came
my mother said
the dog could sleep
on the barley-sugar bed.

He ate it.

Irene Rawnsley

The Pumpkin

You may not believe it, for hardly could I:
I was cutting a pumpkin to put in a pie,
And on it was written in letters most plain
'You may hack me in slices, but I'll grow again.'

I seized it and sliced it and made no mistake
As, with dough rounded over, I put it to bake:
But soon in the garden as I chanced to walk,
Why there was that pumpkin entire on his stalk!

Robert Graves

Have You Heard of the Man?

Have you heard of the man
   Who stood on his head,
And put his clothes
   Into his bed,
And folded himself
   On a chair instead?

Anon.

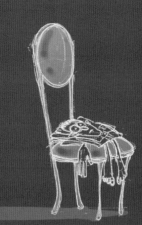

A Mouse In Her Room Woke Miss Dowd

A mouse in her room woke Miss Dowd;
She was frightened and screamed very loud,
   Then a happy thought hit her
   To scare off the critter,
She sat up in bed and meowed.

Anon.

Catapillow

A catapillow
is a useful pet.

To keep
upon your bed

Each night you simply
fluff him up

Then rest
your weary head.

Roger McGough

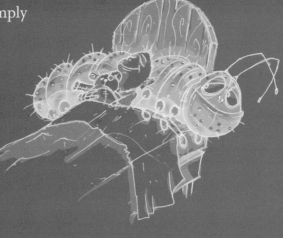

Stargrazing

If the sun were made of birthday cake
I'd eat at least six slices.
If the moon was made of marmalade—
Ah, sweet oranges and spices.

If space was made of lemonade
To swim would be amazing.
If stars were tiny lollipops
I'd spend my night stargrazing.

John Rice

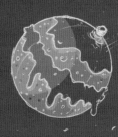

Lullaby

Open your eyes and go to sleep.
The ocean's high. The mountain's deep.
I'll keep you safe from howling sheep,
so open your eyes and go to sleep.

Stand up tall and rest your head.
The star is green. The moons are red.
Sleep safe and sound while I eat your bed.
Just stand up tall and rest your head.

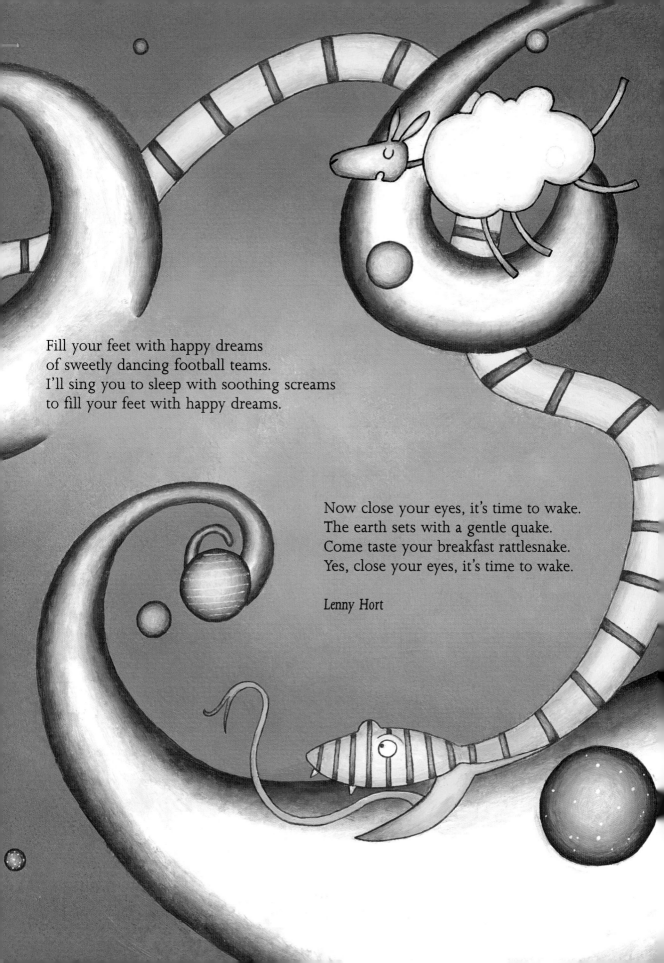

Fill your feet with happy dreams
of sweetly dancing football teams.
I'll sing you to sleep with soothing screams
to fill your feet with happy dreams.

Now close your eyes, it's time to wake.
The earth sets with a gentle quake.
Come taste your breakfast rattlesnake.
Yes, close your eyes, it's time to wake.

Lenny Hort

Index of Titles and First Lines

First lines are in italics

Acknowledgements

We are grateful for permission to include the following poems:

Hilaire Belloc: 'The Bison' from *Complete Verse* (Pimlico, 1991), copyright © The Estate of Hilaire Belloc 1970, reprinted by permission of PFD on behalf of the Estate of Hilaire Belloc; **Charles Causley**. 'Mr Pennycomequick' from *Figgie Hobbin* (Macmillan, 1970), reprinted by permission of David Higham Associates; **Richard Digance**: 'The Ants at the Olympics' from *Animal Alphabet* (Michael Joseph, 1980), copyright © Richard Digance 1980, reprinted by permission of Penguin Books Ltd; **Richard Edwards**: 'Uncle Ted's Tea' from *The Word Party* (Lutterworth, 1986); 'If I Were an Explorer' from *If Only* (Viking Kestrel, 1990); and 'Simple Simon Bought a Pie' from *Nonsense Nursery Rhymes* (OUP, 1997), all reprinted by permission of the author; **Willard R. Espy**: 'My TV Came Down with a Chill' from *A Children's Almanac of Words at Play*, copyright © Willard Espy 1982, reprinted by permission of Clarkson Potter Publishers, a division of Random House, Inc. and Harold Ober Associates, Inc.; **Max Fatchen**: 'Little John was not content' from *Songs for My Dog and Other People* (Viking Kestrel, 1980), reprinted by permission of John Johnson (Authors' Agent) Ltd; **Sheree Fitch**: 'Mabel Murple' from *Toes in My Nose and Other Poems*, copyright © Sheree Fitch 1987, reprinted by permission of the publishers, Doubleday Canada, a division of Random House of Canada Ltd; **Robert Graves**: 'The Pumpkin' from *Complete Poems In One Volume* edited by Beryl Graves and Dunstan Ward (2000), reprinted by permission of the publisher, Carcanet Press Ltd; **Julie Holder**: 'Chester's Undoing', copyright © Julie Holder 1980, first published in *A Second Poetry Book*, edited by John Foster (OUP, 1980) reprinted by permission of the author; **Lenny Hort**: 'Lullaby' from *Tie Your Socks and Clap Your Feet* (Simon & Schuster, 2000), text copyright © Lenny Hort 2000, reprinted by permission of Atheneum Books for Young Readers, an imprint of Simon & Schuster Children's Publishing Division; **X. J. Kennedy**: 'Snowflake Soufflé', copyright © X. J. Kennedy 1975, from *One Winter Night in August* (Atheneum, a Margaret McElderry Book, 1975), reprinted by permission of Curtis Brown Ltd, New York; **Roger McGough**: 'The Midnight Skaters' from *Pillow Talk* (Viking, 1990), copyright © Roger McGough 1990; and 'Catapillow' from *Another Day on Your Foot and I Would Have Died* (Macmillan, 1996), copyright © Roger McGough 1996, reprinted by permission of PFD on behalf of Roger McGough; **Margaret Mahy**: 'The Man from the Land of Fandango' from *Nonstop Nonsense* (J. M. Dent, 1977), reprinted by permission of the publisher, Orion Children's Books; **Andrew Matthews**: 'The Waltzing Polar Bears', copyright © Andrew Matthews 2000, first published in Ivan and Mal Jones (eds.): *Good Night Sleep Tight* (Scholastic, 2000), reprinted by permission of PFD on behalf of Andrew Matthews; **Spike Milligan**: 'On the Ning Nang Nong' from *Silly Verse for Kids* (Puffin, 1968), reprinted by permission of Spike Milligan Productions; **Trevor Millum**: 'Valerie Malorie and Sue Hu Nu', copyright © Trevor Millum 1991, first published in John Foster (ed.): *Twinkle Twinkle Chocolate Bar* (OUP, 1991), reprinted by permission of the author; **Adrian Mitchell**: 'The Gondoliers of Greenland' and 'The elephant knocked the ground' from *Balloon Lagoon and Other Magic Islands of Poetry* (Orchard, 1997), copyright © Adrian Mitchell 1997, reprinted by permission of PFD on behalf of Adrian Mitchell. Educational Health Warning: Adrian Mitchell asks that none of his poems are used in connection with any examination whatsoever; **Cynthia Mitchell**: 'A Frog and a Flea' from *Halloweena Hecatee, and Other Rhymes to Skip To* (Heinemann, 1978), copyright © Cynthia Mitchell 1978, reprinted by permission of Egmont Children's Books Ltd, London; **Peter Mortimer**: 'Bigtrousers Dan' from *The Expanded Utter Nonsense* (Iron Press, 2001), reprinted by permission of the author; **Ogden Nash**: 'Uncle Ed's Heads' ('Fame was a Claim of Uncle Ed's'), copyright © 1953, 1979 Ogden Nash from *Custard and Company* selected by Quentin Blake (Viking Kestrel, 1979), reprinted by permission of Curtis Brown Ltd, New York; **Brian Patten**: 'Uncle Ben from Number One' from *The Utter Nutters* (Puffin Books, 1994), copyright © Brian Patten 1994, reprinted by permission of the author c/o Rogers Coleridge & White Ltd, 20 Powis Mews, London W11 1JN; **Mervyn Peake**: 'My Uncle Paul of Pimlico' from *Rhymes Without Reason* (Methuen, 1978), reprinted by permission of David Higham Associates; **Andrew Fusek Peters**: 'The Dancing Carrot' (traditional Czech), copyright © Andrew Fusek Peters 2002, first published in this collection; **Gervase Phinn**: 'My Cousin, an Explorer Called Betty', copyright © Gervase Phinn 2002, first published in this collection; **Jack Prelutsky**: 'Cincinatti Patti', from *Ride a Purple Pelican* (Greenwillow Books, 1986), © 1986 by Jack Prelutsky, reprinted by permission of HarperCollins Publishers (USA); **Irene Rawnsley**: 'Dog's Dinner' from *Dog's Dinner* (Methuen Children's Books, 1990), copyright © Irene Rawnsley 1990, reprinted by permission of the author; **James Reeves**: 'If Pigs Could Fly', copyright © James Reeves from *The Complete Poems for Children* (Heinemann, 1994), reprinted by permission of the James Reeves Estate, c/o Laura Cecil Literary Agency; **John Rice**: 'Stargrazing', copyright © John Rice 2002, first published in this collection; **Clive Riche**: 'Octopus', copyright © Clive Riche 2002, first published in this collection;

Artists Inside illustrations are by:

Mary McQuillan
10–11, 22–3, 34–5, 48–9,
64–5, 76–7, 88–9.

Chris Mould
12–13, 20–1, 30–1, 37, 42–3,
52–3, 68–9, 74–5, 86–7.

Teresa Murfin
14–17, 40–1, 46–7, 54–5, 63,
68–9, 82–5.

Katie Saunders
5, 26–7, 32–3, 38–9, 56–7,
60–1, 90–1.

Melanie Williamson
18–19, 24–5, 28–9, 44–5, 50–1,
58–9, 66–7, 78–81.

I TO

YOU

OLD

SO!